OVER THE RAINBOW

Copyright © 2022 by Janae Ballard

All rights reserved. No part of this book may be reproduced in any manner whatsoever without written permission except in the case of brief quotations embodied in critical articles and reviews.

Heart of Glory Publishing

www.ballardjanae.com

ISBN: 978-1-7350082-1-9

OVER THE RAINBOW

Over The Rainbow

PROSE AND POETRY

JANAE BALLARD

Heart of Glory Publishing

CONTENTS

1	Revelations	1
2	The New and Worthy Life	17
3	Old Darkness	43
4	Liberation	71

ABOUT THE AUTHOR   143

| 1 |

Revelations

DIVINE INTERCESSION

In six days, the Omniscient
Submitted the world's order to Himself.

Full liberty and predestination.
Full mercy and righteous judgment.

Nature responds in accord—
The ongoing rise and fall of day,
The ongoing rise and fall of
Revelation, justice, and evil;
Nothing new under the sun.

Each generation forgetting lessons,
And that only one remains.
God is infinite, and finite beings fade.
Leaders and teachers taught in vain.
To Him belongs wisdom to be ordained.

And wisdom knows:
Truth sets free,
But *WHO* is truth?
And love wins,
But *WHO* is love?

God's people should remember the seventh day—

Rest in Christ. Rest in God. Rest in the Holy Spirit.
Rest trusting His power and grace, growing richly in
Intercession and prayer; working however He calls,
And embracing the Sabbath.

HOLY TEMPLE

I see my Lord building a temple.

A temple
Undivided,
A temple
Unimpaired.

Since the curtains ripped open
At the death of His Son,
No replacement, except
Of the heart, is accepted.

Nothing unholy enters,
No lies to separate or deter
Full recognition
That purest love dwells therein.

Dark and Light Veilings

The veil of snow lifts
To a winter's mountainside.
A rush of tear crystals,
A breeze of roses white.
The whisper of daises
Caught around the air
Drifts alongside feather clouds
And dandelion wishes.
A disbelieving blink.
A tip-toe of faith.
How much was hidden
Behind the veil of ash?

Nearing Liberty

I've acquired priceless words
Birthed of redemption,
Shaped by wisdom.

Precious grounding stones,
I wish to scatter freely
To spread this firm foundation.

Leveling plains by resonating,
Changing mentalities in conversation.
My mind's acquired such a blessing.

I hear an unseen Spirit speaking of a paradise
Birthed of resurrection,
Made by love.

I hope the heavens sprinkle freely,
So we can walk on promises,
Ascending the fruit tree, and

Climbing rainbow stairs
To taste and see the wonders found
As we get closer to the voice of Christ.

God's Love Story

Thank you for Your life in ink,
The Word, the Book, the love letter.
The window to holy ground,
The illuminating soul reader
That connects creation to Creator.
The non-fiction script.

You wrote of warriors and of brides.
God became flesh,
Your entrance the climax,
To redirect our ending,
And to live abiding in Your open arms,
Sealed away in perfect relations.

Silver Waters

One silver lining there is.

One sliver of hope.

One place to wash our sins.

Sink into the pool of pages.

The *Living Word* is *Living Water*.

Glory to Glory

God keeps His touch upon His art until it's done.
And He orchestrates His beloved's sanctification
    in perfect purpose.
Christ the advocate, our great High Priest,
Seals us for His name's sake, seals our destiny.
Whoever needs His stainless robe, He says, "Share all
    with me."
In the treasuries of His faithfulness—
A spanning sin to repentance, birth to born-again!
From death to life, the dead man's will into reunited
    with the living God!—
I have abided, grown, and grow
Glory to glory.

The great I AM who called my heart to wake
And introduced His love for awe and longing;
The more I grasp of Him, I come to an understanding—
I have beheld and hold a mere fragment
Of all want and satisfaction. I now, by given faith
Believe and see grand creation, my DNA,
And the preexistent all-knowing mind,
Perfect throughout endless time—
He expounds from the highest and will exceed
Glory to glory.

What wonder follows me? By Him, darkness is rid,
And lies which blinded are no longer wounding.
My captivation has found the one redeemer,
Who of unmatched power extends the ability
To walk under sovereign peace. He who connects
The supernatural for us to share His feats.
Through His restoring presence, bloodstained
Lands turnover to holy grounds. By whom
The great kingdom is at hand—earth to heaven—
Glory to glory.

Noah

Like raindrops, voices fall.

Like thunder, their thoughts.

A million taps on the shoulder

Has a billion preoccupied.

Masses scurry in countless directions.

Bump after bump, the push

And brush go by, goes by, goes by.

But, someone amid the crowd stands indifferent,

Solely sensitive to hearing God's command.

Beauty Belongs To...

Beauty belongs to nature.

And its botanical gardens are like a wife in love. She's in love, and she adorns herself—welcomes her bridegroom forward by a blush and wink, with hopes to dance and skip through the night, where once the wind rises with a chill, she can hold him by moonlight eyes and keep him in slumber's silence between mahogany limbs and branches, in the budding softness of her hands, a touch like cherry blossoms.

And nature's mountains would be a man of chivalry—the grandest sight of strength. With edges sharp as armor, admired from afar; yet beckons you closer to lay like snow around its arm, so to know all for discovery at their side, speaks quaking talks of God, His world of worth, everything with heart.

And its sea has made many loves; being fluid, stern, and grace—the love who respects their name before they share or claim another, assuring to give your due value. Uplifts although the capacity to sink. The one who's chosen love because it knows its beauty.

And the open fields, every field of nature—the grasses to

run, the soil to grow on—these carry the most potential, for they give life the land to own, whereby it is cared for,

The heart to whom beauty belongs.

Spiritual Darkness, Spiritual Light

God looks at spiritual darkness,
Spiritual light.

God paints people multicolor,
But right and wrong in black and white.

We are all shades of brown,
Living shades of grey.

God alone is pure;
Humanity cannot equate.

Opposing evils, lies, and distortions,
God brings each lesser form into ruin,

But sets His Son to shine
For illumination.

Christ within a person's heart
Makes them perfect.

Covered by intercession
During judgment,

These now shaded red

Are free.

Though thoughts of "blood-spill"
May plague them,

Their repentance knows
Of rebirth,

Where all is new
And innocent.

| 2 |

The New and Worthy Life

Red Water Faucet

Sin once a cataract,
Now the dripping faucet.
Prayer stopped the rain, but
Christ's return must fix what's broken.

My will to stop the downpour,
By blindness I sip the well;
Deceived to think it living water,
The drip returns instead.

My pang which drains unending.
My fault and drowning distress!
Detestable 'til hopeful tears are salted taste,
Purifying a reminder to wait.

Solely For God

I am the pearl in a clam's mouth.
I am diamonds tucked deep in earth's mantle.
I am the count of flowers in vast fields—
In the petals' hold and go each passing wind.
I am the layers of sand beneath a massive shore.
I am galaxy stars light-years away.
I am the intricacy of snowflakes.
I am something that exists…
Solely for God's glory.

Temptation Is Not Sweet

Temptation is not sweet.
Temptation is the lie
Appearing ripe
To an untrained eye.
But I have savored and seen
Greater love to reach;
A Father's arms to scale
And top the tree.
God is highest;
A love most faithful,
To lift and woo His people
Above low-hanging fruit.

Saved Through Fire

Death is becoming more approachable. To horror or pleasure is life eternal? I turn towards the allure beyond the gate. Do you disdain our conclusion? I admit it. I look death in the face and marvel at the open mouth protruding its tongue of fire. It's inviting. Should I fear being devoured by what I am accustomed? I can go forward in the voice of the harp, find through death's lullaby I wake to my crooning God.

The Movement of Faith

Mountains to move.

Oceans to part.

I'll break and unfold;

You'll enter my heart.

Here, I submit to Your will;

Faith going forward.

Fight the Good Fight

We must fight the good fight,
Faith to faith,
Receiving new mercies every day,
Or the fallen man will take his stand
For our ruin.

We must press on,
Glory to glory,
Recreated consistently in Christ's image;
The old man put to death
For our redemption.

Body Made of Armor

A body made of armor;

Stands in expectation.

Strength for love to strike them,

Without a need of fear.

The silver souls protected

By silver promises;

Their shield against evil,

A sword of confidence.

On Facing Evil

Does God shield eyes from evil?
Or cover death reeked lands of abomination?
No, but He opens them to new desires,
To search out the upward fields of milk and honey.
We can settle in distressing over sights,
But should God revert us to being blind?
No, He says: keep your heart on things above,
And live with fire before His return!
Go, gather the people eager to see!
They are of promise, and promise remains!
No one can turn from the needs of justice
Except to face a righteous judgment.

A Burning Zeal

An eye caught by fire on a bush
Turned a man into a flame.
People knew he had been among God
By the blinding light upon his face.

Who can you liken to the Lord?
The giving Son who gives the moon and stars.

A heart caught by fire in a Spirit
Turned my life into a tree.
Knowledge of good and evil doesn't make a soul a god,
But knowledge of *life* reveals Him to the soul.

What can you liken to the Lord?
What holds all truth before it's told?

Burning pride bleeding over!
The passion inside my soul!
How to resist being consumed
Lest I overflow?

Grounded on the grounds of God,
Rooted in roots from post-creation;

Beholding glory!

I run wildfires
To spread what I am given!
I branch out
To share the fruit I relish!

Be a Child of Israel

Where will you live when the world dies?

I want you beside me
When the searing lies and excuses run dry
After the sun eats every fountain.

During those times of starvation,
Will you be feeding on your tears?
God forbid! I have a home!—

I want you brimming in God's kingdom!

Baptized into Christ;
Divine culture,
My residence!—

Be a soldier alongside me,
Sojourning to the eternal hill, Zion!
Be a child of Israel.

My brother. My sister. Eyes up!

The King in focus;
On Abba, our Father!
Faith high on the expedition.

Those who go under fire
Through water
Are born-again

For their stance on spiritual grounds.

Come now,
Waste not!
I want to see you

Marching with solid eyes,
Which weep only
Of joy.

Divine Venture

>Take the trail!
>Hike the heights we do not know!
>Perhaps, at the top of the mountain,
>>you'll find a way out for us.
>
>Announce what the trees have learned
>>from those at the ending distance!
>
>Search the view at the mountaintop for hope
>>of tomorrow!

You will discover not all will see the peak.

Not all have the strength to venture.

But go if you can! Test the danger! Mark where few have been!

>Remember how we ached and fell asleep
>>in the darkest valley?
>
>You woke nearly dead, rotting head to feet.
>But alas!
>It was a dream!
>It felt as though a warning...

Someone should risk finding life before risking this grave.

Should say goodbye to familiar grounds to go the extra mile.

Can you walk alone and beat the gazing sun; beat the uprising hate?

> It drains the soul of man but not a Spirit set on faith.
> Do not rest in misery.
> Find the promised land!
> Cross over!
> Roll on fertile floors, and do not think of us.

Kick up the soil and cherish life on the other side.

We have but what you maintain. So, be fulfilled

Before you need, seek, to teach of healing.

Moonlit Skin

Nude belongs to moonlight.
Nakedness to love.
What can you say about me
If you have never seen my heart?
The calls after midnight
Are between those I trust.
A sun's lust for life sees all
And reveals too much... but
My skin under moonlight
Never burns.

Mighty Prince

I wish to be a mighty fighter!
A great warrior in battle armor.
A cherished son by the Father,
Who conquers death, gains life eternal.
My Lord of Holy War,
      The Kings of kings—
Bringing all under dominion.
My Lord of Vengeance,
      The God of Justice—
Clothe me down in sword and shield!
If I come to bear bruises by enemies,
Or by a swipe of blood, I am made faint,
Even then, find me at Your side!
Carry me to Your victory!

Still, Small Voice

My molecules are speaking
In ways I cannot hear.
All over there are words
Written but unclear.
And it's strange, feeling blind,
Although knowing more.
But mysteries uncovered,
I keep them close and dear.
Then share and select secrets.
I tell, yet resolve some silence.
For, what is hard to understand
And not plain to see sounds like
An upper hand or an underlying threat
To those who will not listen to
Still and small voices who
Talk this way as from a place of peace.

Bestowed a Crown

Here is a crown that moves only by the holder's touch;
Bestowed and sealed to thee and the heavens.
It draws upon the head a walk of high shoulders;
Remains in splendor and position while allowing bows,
Low in full submission, to the Lord our God.
A crown gifted in a world of poverty. Wear it
Delighting to serve! Honor and responsibility, like that
Of your Father, King's is your selflessness.
Your treasuries are your people.
With these, we share our heart and riches.
But there is ridicule, envy over Love's throne;
Those who desire to rule, not in peace but power.
Do not retreat when they seek to take the crown.
Rather demand law is upheld, and show evil's sufferings.
Yes, mercy's given after their recognized defeat.
We fall only in removing our crowns in deceit.
So know who you are, and pride in your royalty.

It Is Out of My Hands

Farwell.
You will not be sulked.
What has slipped through fingers
Is better off;
My failure to keep,
Farewell.
I nor my head will fall.
I am held.

Those Who Love God Have Loved Me

How sweet,
Sincerest brethren
Well-taught in our shared beliefs.
Those who honor God have honored me.

How sweet,
The reminder to have faith.
Those who love God have loved me.
His grace surrounds. It's true to save.

Wayside Fare

Wayside child,
Milked of delight,
Mere shadow sitting black and grey;

Lost in a haze,
Stuck by the drain,
The person of rain

Swallowed.
Promise returns color to life.
The light of God restarts the hope.

Wayfaring stranger,
Known in heaven,
Please, return to Him.

Red washed streams
Float in His hand,
Readily pouring life.

Wayfaring child,
Gone without restraint
Believing outside imitations...

Now is both the muffled hour and the time to drink.

Please, wayside child, do not abandon God,
Rather the world's pollution.

Tolls and Trades

Either we win together,
Or you've lost.
Hatred pays its toll.
Ever since your failed desire
Succeeded in my hand,
Your resentment burns.
But I do not fear hell's devices.
Why unravel yourself
While I am clothed?
Besides mercy, what is kept?
Love trades beauty for ruins.

Baptism

Water's cold, but not this light.
The lower the step, the higher the rise.
Drowning what's old, embracing new life.
The chill is piercing, the warmth is right.
Like an innocent womb forming a mind;
Though fully aware before opening eyes
To leave the darkness there.

| 3 |

Old Darkness

Better Adam

I prove time and time
I am true to the human race;
In its corruption, fallen nature,
And fickle mistakes.
But it is then I boast again,
Being within the significant rank,
Of God's sufficient grace.

Unless He Intercedes

Where can I put my trust?
Not in my righteousness.
Even to put my hope in God,
I tarry in the task.
Oh, I tarry.
I tarry.
I try and doubt.
Who will come and rescue me?
I misconstrue His heart.
Unattainable perfection,
Highness unfathomable;
I waver, but He's unchanging,
Faithful despite my part.
I believe and tarry.
I tarry to believe.
Oh, I die
Unless
Christ maintains
Assurance of salvation.

Pleads of Promise

Pain pleads a testimony: A hate.
Glory pleads for remembrance: Await.
    God sees.
    God weeps.
    God brings healing.
Patience pleads of promise, and pain testifies against
Being hurtful, being forgetful. God's glory waits
For faith. But not forever, not always
At the expense of hatred in His children
Dearly loved and understood.

Spiritual Hauntings

I use to be so afraid of my mind. Not anymore...
But would I recommend opening the door to
Countless questions I questioned before?
Bats hanging and winging under cave beam hours.
Both God and life can seem pretty haunting.
Blood spills and true agonies,
Do they make a mockery of mercy?
God pours wrath on those tainting His innocence,
In word or deed, spirit or "truth," or the cruel "mistake."
Death and death read on my brain,
The first, the second tortures.
Shells of a love deceived to living hell
By unknown shadow figures.
But God is salvation true. Go look evil in the eyes;
Fear is bound to lie. Don't turn away in vanity;
Aren't we running out of time? The threat is not so scary
If your ghost is holy. Knowing Jesus saves,
He can control the mind with grace.

Heavenly Father

The fears of waking to a father dead;
God, You sweep away such agonies of love.
I wake to the sun instead, to light, to bliss;
Heaven's shelter and everlasting estate.
I, a heart, outflowing greater measures
Than the days before. My anticipations
Met by sovereign peace again.
Father, You proudly look after me.
Father, inform my earthy father,
My mother, my brother; inform the world,
Family truly lasts forever in Your sphere.

Conversion

Behind me is the unfolding of the most horrific day of history—

Every tree has split and fallen, buildings concaved, and winds blow about dangerous debris. The sky is beyond bleak, grey, and dusty, as souls run about for shelter nonexistent. Grounds shift and shake. Earthquakes break and swallow so much of the land I forget the reason we ever thought it a firm foundation for our lives, our homes, our dreams. Screams and crying, scenes of cemeteries crumbling start to blind me in the blood of my heart racing. And I need light. A spark for my eyes! Thus quickly, I lead myself toward the hope of such a find, and nearby... one flashing object ahead, though faint, blacking out I leap for it.

Then awake—

Standing on a path with no beginning, simply a road winding far to an ending my gut insists is present despite my inability to see it. I look behind. Seeing a steep cliff and that everything surrounding it is pitch black I turn forward to this path which could be my future. Bright and peculiar. I glance back again. Utter darkness. A feeling dreadfully counter-nostalgic, as though watching a memory—the destruction of my past, of the world I knew last. No going back. All is surpassed and collapsed by the hand that brought me here.

Appears...

I have met a new life. And I can never see the old without remembering death.

Timer: Divine Timing

Trapped inside an hourglass horror,
The fleeting of time falls to quote an infinity—
A hundred years per grain of sand,
Of drowning in brimstone lakes.
Cold sweat erupts at the thought.
The evil in the heart,
Destructive heart.
Weakness
And sin
Would
Take
Who
There!?
A suicide
Pours upon
The back, bargains
For life! Grinds into foreshadowed
Ash. Dust. Dust. "Life's end." Time ticks.
Out breaks a call for freedom! Glass breaks,
And meet the *Author of Time* on a frozen shore,
A stilled tide. Salvation, alive before death.

Out Of The Pit

Not all at once my becoming lost.
Step after step in the wrong direction.
Taking advice from imperfection.
Followed my way into a hole.
A murky place where no relief could come,
Where I heard people singing "inspiring" songs
(Nothing feeling sincere or alive.) No true rescue,
Until a passerby, who refused to be a passerby.

Terrifying seeing Him look at me.
Holes in both His hands and feet.
He, Himself, though radiant had suffered the world too.
A recollection of why I no longer thought to move
And would not aimlessly wander again. He called,
His first words, directing me to "faith".
But it did not encourage.
I questioned why should I believe anything,
Everything unexciting and incomplete...
But He, a relentless type, reached with strength enough
To pull me up despite my desire and countless woes
Which surprisingly bothered only me. I would plead,

"There is no sunshine bright enough to put a fire in my heart.

There is no ocean wide enough to convince me I will see better days whereon my sorrow won't put it to shame.

There is no dream I could accomplish to shake me awake to boast in life.

I am in a deadly sleep, fitting of the pit."

> But gently hushed, I was told of someplace unseen.
> Where those feelings of despair could not even
> Be imagined. Explained He was taking me there,
> And how I could have it freely. And though I
> Did not accept it, I noticed in my chest an awe,
> A beating of memories, of laughter, and the love
> Experienced before the cave and mire. And I was
> Impressed by the reminder, though fleeting.
> It caused a thought, that just maybe...
>
> A place—where grief's destroyed, as well as it's made
> Here. Just maybe, and having to know I stopped
> Pulling down and joined in climbing. Then noticed
> The world was already changing, already far under me.
> That I was actually experiencing liberation and heading
> Somewhere made of grace, for me, by Him.

Ear to Hear

I prayed to You as a child without burden,
Yet grew to wonder if sin severed our connection.
I needed God and prayed with no hesitation.
And one day, somehow so empty, all my sin I abandoned.
Then You spoke to me outside of prayer
Through messengers and a letter.
I hoped You loved me then, I know it now!
You went every length to redeem our relations.
Behind the scene, other principalities and dominions
Tried to claim my fallen soul for their keeping.
Although I lived a life that gave them reason
Having found peace in evil,
You saw their love was for my destruction
And pitied what I settled for.
Though "happily" taken, You fought Your mocker
And reclaimed me.
My uncertainties were due to sin,
But You took this upon Your shoulders to
Walk and talk with me side by side.
Now, You answer every prayer,
Not always with a "yes" but of Your nature.
I am finally introduced to Your character.

My Dismissal

You don't understand.
I felt it in my bones, white;
Disembodied.
"Inadequate Matter"
It passed right through me;
The way of dismissal.
I will not be seen,
I am a ghost, dead,
Drifting through life,
Apart from skin. But,
This isn't true.
Groan for groan,
I am heard like you.
I am here. I am present
Among the inhumane,
Aware that God can exhale
And we be wrought alive.
I'm supposed to be overtaken
By life's cruelty.
You don't understand
This mentality of mine,
The impossible, a miracle.
I'm supposed to be gone.
Every breath I take is God.

Prophetic Dreams

In a moment of a dream, God could paint a prophecy—the offering fulfilled in Christ—across a foreign mind and over the world I look upon and ask, "Has there been grace?" for.

How have I entered this place in time, under the scope and close watch of God's eye, crying in my hands without stop until He lifts my head to the hands of the clock?

He looks upon me with well intent, delight, and love; I am His child of faith

aching at the thought of people aging away into darkness, rejecting light.

But none wants association with what could cost a pleasure. For, He has written "God" on our lips, but we toss truth away, undesired in pride, to build an idol for service, or to be our own "god".

I see the righteous judgment, but let it not be so. Though I know mercy is injustice when evil does not reap what it's sown, when liars escape confusions caused, when no one suffers for all that is lost... Jesus bleeds! May His glory be known; it's on our behalf! May it be known that God has come down in the flesh!

"Send me I'll go!"

The time ticks aloud.
Seems to strike the hour, word for word.

"Lord, will You keep patient as I speak?"

"Go with haste!" He says to me,
"Honest. And it will be, as in a moment of a dream.
Some have gone, but many remain asleep."

Eraser

Memories
That sit on skin
And leave it stained
As hands by sin,
These too
Will be washed away,
Pure white
As the blood of Christ
Is in the eyes of God
Which have watched
Over all of time.

Devil's Advocate

A tongue of fire
Exists in your mouth,
A split tongue of fire.

You tore me apart
With God's good word.
You burned me like a devil.

The light you bore,
You used for harm,
Divided truth incorrectly.

Condemning tone,
No way from hell,
You left me in confusion.

You came in bright,
Came clever lies;
You got your lick and beat me—

To never rise,
To never know
The Love you'd never spoken.

Weight of Glory

The weight of glory is worth all things...
But the heaviness as of late
Could pull tears from the most hardened warrior
Who hasn't wept in years.
Burdensome
This fight against
Great depravity.
I tire every hour,
But war and battle call of me.
So, I clothe myself in armor,
The nauseous weight of every piece.
Though weariness and ills at hand,
I grip my sword with grace.
"Victory, Victory!"
I strengthen my soul with shouts!
A bruised man is unsightly,
But *this* also stirs my heart;
As every fall,
Every sin,
Conquered underfoot
Makes me rise to the weight of glory,
Which lifts me!
Lifts me up!

Weathering Together

Have You heard that You're beautiful in the middle of a storm?
        Told, "You can bring Your thunder,"
        And "You can bring Your flood."?

        I will dance in gratitude to surprise You;
            I only fear skies without Your presence.
You are loved through the rain, and when You're the black cloud.

        Guardian of the meek, slow me down for worship!
Love, more than worthy, is known beneath Your wing.
            Will I reject my shelter because of weatherings?

Cynicism

Cynicism comes with guilt feelings, and weight in hearing truth in what you speak.
It'll fall on you like thick curtains, shutting out all light. But darkness is not what you tried to bring.
Fear that you've pondered into underground wonders, wrap you in a mental grave.
But you're not dead yet, you fight for the hope in your chest, and pray that it won't cave.
Your faith is tested and you start to doubt the world which you see.
You know so little but your sadness, and so enter into grief.
Your tears become a salty storm, a night of no relief.
A wait on God to show His Son who too by evil was buried—
Yet not overtaken. A living steady shelter, who by His light destroys what is unclear and bleak.

The Carrier

Bags on eyes carrying cries
    Not my own.
Head aching with worries
    Not my own.
Heavy shoulder of sadness
    Not my own.
A slouch and groan
    I have learned.
Ceased laughter, hard-hearted;
    Being dead before I'm gone.
But it is only for a time,
    At the end, it will be forgotten.
If I can focus
    Ahead
I can carry confidence;
    A heart breaking out in song,
An encouraging and reproving—
    A light on a hill—
God's light.
    Not my own.

Wrath and Love

God is against me
and there is no love.

This explains why my crying threatens to
overtake me, like a sea that won't let up,
like the ocean He could dry up
if He weren't drowning me.
God has already thrown me into darkness,
and there will be no salvation.

I wander for light
in a hopeless world.

"Follow me." He says.
Isn't it mockery?
He knows no strength is in my feet.

"Believe. I will help you," He says,
knowing my faith is dead.
I was born to die in disparity.

Weeping, I awaited His wrath. And I could feel the heat stirring in. I want to run from His face and hide from His power. But His reality cannot be avoided.

I was woven to be His enemy. "Give me a second chance! I believe." I grieved. I begged Him for mercy, doubting it'd change anything. Then came *lightning*, and I knew I'd be stricken.

"So you believe in My wrath but not in My love?"
He speaks.

I respond,
"I know that's the reason I'll perish."

**"If so,
I could have killed you yesterday..."**

"You're stacking the reasons you should torment me. Letting me frustrate you in disbelief."

Then He called me a ***fool***, and I knew that I was...
Was imbalanced, and running from grace.
Ignoring His Son and making Him into a liar
instead of my corrupted thoughts.
Subjecting to my mind which couldn't discern,
and to which He objected,

**"Count your breath as salvation.
I'll give you a sign. "**

My impatience would hold it in wait.
For how long? Thought I'd die by the night, but

I'd wake miraculously breathing grace

And remembering my ways cannot make Him unfaithful.
Maybe I'll falter, but He won't fail.
He'll fulfill His words and save in due time.

For now, I must rest in the wonder and promise.
Later the revelation.
Faith is simply the truth confessed with the heart,

Confessing the Christ to come.
He will come and remove the confusion
and humble the earth, just as He humbled me.

What Matters

You haven't made too many mistakes to be seen in a different light.
   You don't have to plead your cause.
   A human can be so many things they never wished to.

You don't have to defend yourself
Against everything trying to steal your pride
And victory in Christ.

Sure, answer questions when they're sincere,
Even go the distance. But that's easy.
That's enjoyable, not the voices of hypocrisy.

None of them change anything.
You don't have to handle each offense.
None of it matters in the end,

All that does is living
Free—
As grace is given freely.

What matters is the peace,
The love, the hope, the charity,
And righteousness budding in your new life.

What matters is growing in Him, in going with Him
Day and night; through the skeptics' war and hate
To restoration and paradise.

| 4 |

Liberation

Genuine Happiness

God, You proved peace to exist
When You made joy evident.
Now, I delight in the pleasure of Life,
In genuine happiness.

I look at my smile and
Overhear my laughter.
I can taste my gladness and
Sense how it all comes naturally.

Melodies move, words weave,
Earth enchants, strangers speak,
Creatures connect, families form,
Interests ignite; it's the norm...

Yet my heart is touched into reaction
Captured to breathe with satisfaction
And this... this is bliss! How
Favor follows and grace persists

For genuine happiness.

The Pieces Will Fall Together

The pieces will fall together one by one, 'til *it's* done.
All the broken brought together;
All that's worn, all that's torn.
All that wrought in shambles, and mightily held through
For a child, for a sibling, for a future, for fear…

The pieces will fall together one by one, 'til *it's* done.
All evils brought low,
All sly and vicious, all betrayal.
All unhinging those undiscerning humbled at exposure,
    judged to their core
Against the innocent, against justice, against peace and
    mercy.

The pieces will fall together one by one, 'til *it's* done.
All the righteous brought honor,
All pleasure, all rewarded in the Lord;
All, "Well done, good and faithful servant. *It* is finally
    finished,
Receive the kingdom, receive healing, receive love in
    perfect form."

What You Gave

Bitter tears roll over bitter stones scrapping my feet in a forgotten garden.

Thought the bag of seeds and watering can were my rights to a green thumb...

Accepting harvest comes by grace, not labor. Oh, so, I must be still and sleep!

The value of mercy didn't increase overnight but over the weeks of wait.

Finally, the grape took to my tongue and it was refined in taste.

Divine enough to serve the Lord when I thought solely to feed the hungry.

But His order, His center focus, is the single chance of being fruitful.

Only in Your provision, in time, we reap a satiating drop of heaven.

Lifted

Do you feel lifted with the raising of the sun—
With the hum, the song of the bird?
There is a reason you are alive!
I hope you know!
Whether to do or inspire something great,
Glorious purpose! Do rise to the occasion.
Live with love.
So many are told differently.
So many are aching.
Be quick to forgive them.
Though they may aim directly,
None of it's personal.
Give without expectation. Give without approval.
Though skeptics and hatred may arise,
The Son is also lifted high.
The Son knows your life.
The Son knows.
The Son knows.
The Son knows your purposed life
And has kept you awake under the light.

God: The Purest Friend

God, You found me
And hid me in Yourself.
Meeting You was taking heaven's hand
And rising to cloud 9.

Oh, I am smothered in love by the softest hands
Kneading my shoulders,
Lifting my burdens;
The lightest yoke,

As You carry the world for me...
As You gift a world to me...

Vessel

I have been inspired by the misfit pieces, by
Crooked vessels pouring out refreshment.
Moses is evidence that they serve a purpose.
Filled and chosen through their weakness.
Toss not those with blemishes.
If the world counts you out, don't hear their vision.
You will not break if being held by God;
Though you may crack, you will not fall.
Your doubtfulness makes Him no less faithful to
Carry out His promises, from consequence or discipline
Unto His glory and child's redemption.

Gracious King

God, am I trustworthy?
I know myself for pride;
I could be a thief of glory.
Why lay Your jewels before me?

May dress myself in Your splendor;
Name myself a goddess.
I'm no leader for praise,
Scared to carry the burden;

Scared to betray the true throne,
Building castles on ruin.
This world's not my home,
Neglect it and Your love...

Crooked royalty of my very own impeachment.
Some power and privilege can cover the weakest.
If queen, in a tower of stumbling blocks unless
Your power and promise cover the weakest heart.

Awakening!

The sweetest sunlight calls to me,
"Time for an adventure!"
I love daybreak's hour;
A spark of newfound freedom.
Life is well and beautiful
If you're looking up.
While the world can do evil,
Only good is from above.
Someone needs a heavy rain,
Rejoice it restores them.
Intake the sunny days
Being warmed, reflective!
But do awake; rise and shine,
Something bright starts in!
Go as faithful as the darkness ends.

Daughter of Abraham

My Lord gives me a breathtaking promise,
As though I, too, am called to search the stars
And capture all of them.

I also look forward to something
Fitting just for me, made wholly by those same hands
Which spread space for my home in the heavens.

The Light Kept On

I see how God kept me,
Like a new day in His hands.
Fresh sunlight appears clearly;
New mercy, another chance
To bask humbly tasting life—
True opposite of death—fulfills
A desperate soul—precious
As the dying's fleeting words;
Salvation where it had been lost
Had been unheard,
I have.

Black Sheep

You were taken as a babe from the kingdom.
Raised in wilderness' belly.
A lost little lamb, a stray sheep,
Amongst wolves, no shepherd.
Death certain; how soon, unknown.
But the land became your abode.
Grew accustomed to the humdrum:
Howls, late cries, and fear.
Until you ran for isolation,
Stumbled in shadowed woods.
Stuck in grime and grim,
Blackening your wool,
'Til by your broken whimper
A Savior drew near.
Reinstating you in His temple,
A part of the sheepfold,
Beside 99 others, who made you feel
His satisfactory, and finally home.

Record of Love. Cord of Doubt.

Sin wounds love.
      Love wounds sin.
In a tug of war against your Father,
Are you far from giving in?
Does not your desperation afflict your hand?
Has your heart yet to fall over
In a painful belly laugh?
Rebuke is not against you.
It disciplines your Judas;
It overcomes the betraying *"friend."*

Give God His handle on evil.
Let Him do what He pleases.
He strives against your separation;
A redeemer over wrath—
He is not for your destruction.
Cast away rebellion's pain.
What He pulls down is for your discovery
Of His peaceful heart.
Drop the woven doubt
In perfect love.

Raise Up!

    UP! is the direction,
    If I can testify,
In where to lead a child.

    Why leave it to chance, guesses, or assumptions?
    Christ warns of danger as a sovereign guide.

    The Light unto feet,
    Empowering,
When fear binds from all movement.

    He'll take us forward in the treasuries of His heart
    And raise us in true majesty.

Spin-Off

All you need is a promise
In the threat of disaster.
In high winds and reports
Of nearing terror,
All you need is a promise
Countering the claim
To step aside and laugh.

Free!

I'm a free man walking around!

I know what life's all about!

I've got it figured out!

I could see you free from doubt!

Drinkers

A cavern roped and bound restrains water.
The desperate nearly break it—pulling, thirsting.
But gentle hands drew to loosen and unknot
The binding; and insert a filter of special acquiring.
Then by the sober stranger, the needy knew
The purest drink.

Voice of Thunder

Sometimes you need
A voice of thunder,
A roaring lion,
A great defender.
Power fearless
For the weak
Who has rights
And authority.
A King of kings
Against armies;
An earthquake or
Heaven's rumbling.

Because God...

    Because God has filled these lungs to breathe,
I will participate in life.
Today, I will build by hope;
See the future in a better light.
Depressions air and feelings drift.
Could it be left behind?
Even tears, in God's kingdom, reap a joyful harvest.

I will dream again in this miraculous time.
I will picture what could be on the other side.
I will tell someone willing to listen.
I will encircle myself with affirmation,
And not cease trying to find these people.
And once they're known, I will not let them go.
So perhaps, sometimes, I will need some time alone
To relearn values worthy of giving,
To recenter, and gain my footing.
So where I go won't slip away, but be firm, purchased,
And mine; an investment in what surpasses,
A heart for you to safely live forever inside,
In wisdom gained by eyes kept on heaven
From where God spoke and told my soul:
To live is Christ to die is gain.
Everything is pure for the pure at heart.

To seek Thy kingdom come.
So whether pain or pleasure, His glory is reason enough.

Never Alone

Lonesome liar,
Can't you see?
I've been crafted carefully.
Embedded with emotion,
Made for another,
Love is with me.
I am never alone.
Yes, trace me back to Love.
How deep it runs inside me!
I'm in association with a Potter,
Carved in intricate detail.
Now, your lies they cut they do...
But I'm not far removed, as you.
Maybe a solo vessel on the shelf,
But I have yet to fall from grace.

Throne Room

My Lord is a lovely fragrance.
With Him, I sit and breathe fresh air.
His presence rests my senses.
I hope it's clung to me to wear.
Then drifts you into serenity,
Into this blissful, faithful essence.
An aroma full of healing,
Grace consuming mists of blessing.
Inhaling pleasure. Exhaling prayer—
Your entrance in the throne room,
For eternal delight together.

The Depth of My Spirit

The pit in my throat
Silently sings
The richest cord of thanksgiving.
The tears in my eyes
Silently cry
Out of the depth of my Spirit,
As all I am
Operate to come
To terms with salvation.

Supreme magnificence—
The late dimensions of Your beauty!
New earth! New heavens! Paradise in perfection.

I am perfected, a new creation—able to lift proper reverence, sense you, and evolve. Center of the purest place discovering Your endless hand, Your endless heart—unwrapping life eternal for the scope of my footprints.

Your fingerprint,
Your touches,
Intimate;
Your presence
Nearest
Satisfaction—

The tears in my eyes an infinite stream. I know the softest ground,
The smoothest light,
The deepest worship—
The pit in my throat.

Revival

Run quickly, softly, across the cloudy sky of dreams.
Reach down north to south, west to east,
And pull together the land in unity.
Shake the scene 'til idols crumble into extraneous sand.
We will surely weep a little with all that's
Passed through our grasp.
But then in desperation, we'll marvel at each hand.
Look up and ask God, "For these
Did you have plans?"
Then we'll spring up in His laughter,
Working anew in pure zeal and love.
Tending to our talents for the beauty of His world.
Taking pride in ourselves, taking pride in one another;
Rejoicing with worship at His endless glory,
Endless purpose, endless life.
We'll run quickly, softly, under the cloudy sky
In our dream reality.

Communions and Feasts

There is life in blood, unlike the water here, so I will drink from the veins of my Lord.

It may get messy. I may be judged. But He has made this sacrifice for us and I won't allow a drop to be spilled.

What can fill me but my Savior?

This life He gives saves from death.

When I break He takes my brokenness and exchanges His strength for my weaknesses.

He's crushed Himself into pieces to share with me something I cannot ruin.

A power I can taste…

Rising from starvation,

Devouring

The empowerment of this love.

I take

Of His flesh like a meal for my energy.

Weren't we invited to a feast for our unity?

I'm foreshadowing…

Peacemaker

Whilst riding into glory I beg for a mist—a touch of heaven on the earth; a taste of rain, of graciousness that revives the soul to live and birth forward crops of great delight and humble heart from corrupt to right way of passage, path, direction, of peace—Maker, as I go.

Made More

You are more.
More than riches.
More than poetry.
More than who they say.
More than what you think.

You are divine.
Your capacity can embrace more.
More love, more hope, more faithfulness, and life.

Scales

The scales tip in God's favor.
Place your weight in gold against Him.
One drop of blood, His representative,
Sends your end flying through the heavens.

"Of course "blood" prices more than gold," you
Call your family in. They sit on the scale, and
God offers another rich red drop of His own.

Your family is now in God's domain,
Good thing; He knows not to gamble them.
They are of irreplaceable value, *BUT*
So is the blood that bought them.

What will you bring to match Him?
What is the highest gain?
Gather every murderer or gather every saint,

Gather blood from guilty hands,
And claim, "I have saved the world!"
Three drops of blood from God,
And look how much is gone.

If God should die, the whole world does,
Both corrupt and honest.

All belongs to Him, all joy and resurrection.

No other seeks out faultless justice;
No one but Him guarantees it.
No other extends pure, righteous love;
No one but Him can grace it.

One Savior rules the scales, He of
Immeasurable worth. But the scales on eyes,
Fail to count the price on where you stand.

Over The Rainbow

There is a promise kept
Supplying the greatest wealth.
A covenant claimed in faith
By a child of Abraham—

A spiritual inheritance and
Healing of the physical.
A new earth and heaven,
Over the rainbow.

Over the rainbow lyes God's kingdom,
Where man and beast know freedom,
With peace to love and worship the lamb
Whose blood reclaimed the chosen people.

There is a *Living Hope*
Sustaining the broken soul,
Answers riches sought in prayer
With more than temporal gold;

The rarest sight and reign
In a land of praise and color.
The red of Mercy's heart,
In place beyond the veil.

There is a promise kept

Away from sin's deception—
A truth and home to visit,
Though many never will.

Perfect the curiosity;
Lead sorrow to repentance.
Financial gain and poverty
Sift toward the truest Spirit.

Sunsets and days of roaring rain
May miss the final portrait,
But rest your crown in heaven
Under rainbow coverings.

Under the rainbow,
Found hidden in the heart
A pleasure cultivated,
A harvest set apart

From where leaders dictate
Evolution's green and flow.
And without an *Eternal Hand*,
By fear, corruption grows.

The character of society
Should multiply God's image;
Restore the Garden of Eden
From the fallenness of life.

Begin
> Again
>> Instead,

At the end of the rainbow.

There is a *Faithful One*,
His name resounding through the world—
If heard, who believes and
Reaps treasuries above?

Despite not having seen
Out from perversity,
Where misery ceases searching,
Belief affords escape—

Opens pearly gates
Guarding golden streets.
Christ purposes glory in His holiness.
In Him, garments washed in bleeding *Light*.

There is *Living Water*
Shining fruit and keeping favor;
Adds blessing to potential,
Maintains *Love* upon the throne.

He, everlasting, fulfills
> The
> Promised

Land.

God is Enough

God is enough;

As enough as a glass is filled by a waterfall.
As enough as there is room to swim in the ocean.

My thirsting soul needs only Him.
He is pure water to drink, a flood of love,
And *true* love is more than enough.

Fool's Gold

I stumbled upon God's wisdom.
I stumbled and God pitied me.
Found all my hopes to be worthless,
Found myself fallen on my face; and
His pity enriched the fool,
Redeeming old gold to eternal value.

Pour Into Yourself

Pour God's love into yourself
Until it gives you grace for change,
Until it gives you peace and pride,
Until it gives you love like His.
Pour God's love into yourself
Until every cranny which
Makes you feel forgotten is
Overflowing with tender kindness.

Love's Appearance

I peer into a river
Where the sun overlaps my face.
Knowing light is with me,
I go radiant;
Skipping over rocks,
The way the river runs,
Fulfilled once then twice
When a person peeps and sees me.
Their eye within my eye,
Like sky lacing a stream;
God's heart shines from heaven,
Going with us by a glimpse,
Telling 'love is near'.

Miracles Born

I could not choose to be.
This happened miraculously.
Yet who am I that I can choose
       To continue?
  And who are we?
  That you and I choose to be
  And choose to continue life
       Miraculously?
    Or perhaps not so,
    For who are we
    Without these
        Constant miracles?

"Already forgiven"

      Sin brought a wedge between souls
Who'd never encounter again.
But God would have their union restored.
Though the regretter of mistakes expects a grudge
From one so callous when two parted—
Presuming anger keeps the other
From ever seeing them any different—
An apology was discovered at the foot of the cross.

      In a day of seeking God's forgiveness,
On the common grounds of prayer,
Whether there it was sought or whether God was saying
Eventually, you'd hope for that surrender,
It was realized, we all can only pray for having grace.
And what was wanted, is given as received.

Subsiding Terror

Enclosed by thickets and blinded by thorns,
Every thought of moving forward dreadful.
Covered in the dark, hidden from the morn;
Your sight and labor detrimental.

You bled my sin and shame. In distress, I did not reach.
Then when You died my fears stood clearly...
Until Your *Ghost* came to me, a sudden great relief,
And bore a rose from my subsiding terror.

Redeeming Love

Out of bad relationships
Into redeeming love!
Love is not unreasonable.
Love does not cause harm.

Love does not leave you in lies;
Love has a thoughtful mind,
Love desires frequent joy.
Out of bitter times and cries!

Out of lust and interruption,
Into pure admiration!
Love has eyes for all of you;
Love is not blind, but patient.

Love has heard your heart singing;
Love seeks deep connection.
Love is very curious to
Out your laughter and affection.

Out the hidden talents!
Love opens to share its life.
Love gives time to charity.
Love imagines the fun of being kind.

Love will not mock your blemishes;
Love humbly talks and plans.
Love protects your future together
Out into the extraordinary!

Trembling Still

Lord, should You release my hand
It'd shake my very world apart.
I'd take a hold of You again,
Though trembling every moment.
For, "Dare I claim another fill, of grace?"
You still me from such stolen thoughts.

Greater Love

Who could love unless love existed?

Who could laugh unless inspired?

Every good comes from greater.

My good has come from *Greater Love*!

Faithful To Fragility

    Fragile frames
Cannot hold the mass of love.
But love shares a glimmer of its spirit.
A patient and excitable glimmer,
Zealous to stretch; and would shine
In endless perfection if we were not
Such a fragile frame—
Our dependency on mercies,
Having needs to be sustained.

    Our fragile frame is not repellant.
Dear love is kind and reaches to uphold us.
Dear love is gentle and smiles
Even toward the glimmer.
Dear love does not think less of any love,
Knowing it is sacred and is immensely precious.

    But the children's bliss was sacrificed for toiling,
When who thought love to be better deserved?
To chase and weigh our favor
Has led to inner shame and loathing.
We sold our rights of grace,
Abandoning what was known
In deciding we state each cause.

    Dear love returns to me,
To uncover what was wrong.
We both of humility—
Though I barren and soiled of further good—
Dear love does not think less of any love.
Dear love holds me faithfully as if my body were its own.

Bed of Wisdom

The *Bed of Wisdom* drifts

Along consuming depths,

Along the *Sea of Light*

Outshining every void.

Heart of the sea,

Full of *truth*,

Allow an anchor;

Cast away the weight upon a shoulder.

Consume it now by the strength of *grace*;

Shed and wash the hurt and teary face,

Sound asleep on your *Sea of Love*.

Whisperings

Seeping down the family tree is a hissing. Through Father Adam, I hear a serpent's whisper. I hear the whisper of a Covenant through Father Abraham. I hear the whisper of fulfillment through God the Father saying, "Love became flesh," And "walked among us with the promise of salvation for His People. He tramples over evil." The whisper runs in historic Take, travels God's footsteps, since beginnings, where the Whisper given Father Adam is the serpent ruling lies; and By sin I receive them, or by faith dismiss death's bite for life.

When The Impossible Happens

If by a prophet's call,
Rain ascends into the clouds
Would the impossibility introduce God?
Or would you break the scientific order
And act as though it is not supernatural
To the structure of nature?
I say my tears are lifted by *Living Hope*.

Do you not see God restrains the fall?
And how logically He's answered
A believer's broken prayer.

Dear Precious Light

Dear Light,

    Roll in again
    And revive our souls.
    You grace both wise and fools.
    Everyday,
    You seek to interrupt
    The oblivious slumber of man.

    Forbearing
    The cases of death,
    Foreknowing
    Some will rise.
    You persist for resurrection;
    In spite of the abominable amount of decay.

    You bleed,
    Oh, precious sun,
    Weary and fury.
    Your tears could burn us,
    Boil us, oh precious sun,
    Forever.

    But rather you retreat
    By happenchance the sweep of night

Would make notice of Your absence.
Here now, and many have shuddered
Out of the personal nightmare;
And sought and sought to pray in your return.

Oh, precious sun,
When you are witnessed after sorrow
You dry our faces and warm our spirits.
You roll in again
As a blanket of dawn!
And we make our way home.

As you come over the horizon,
You stretch the days of our life.
You are the reason for sincere "Good morning."
Oh, precious sun, never leave again!
Those who know you, beg of you!
Oh unless... we fall asleep.

On Our Train of Thought

No matter how much everything changes—
Societal peer pressures and technological advances—
Certain things remain the same... Right being right,
Wrong being wrong, truth being truth,
False being false, opinions being opinions.
It's liberating honestly; discovering how illuminated
We can be through the fog, above the steam, and
Beyond the loaded train full of passengers going
God knows where. And through a quiet prayer
Can learn if we should board or bid goodbyes.

The Blood In Your Eyes

A shadow casts behind your eyes,
A photo in black and white,
Appearing like a silhouette,
Your mind stands in the way of the light.
And though your heart seems disconnected,
By your stone-cold actions, I look at you and know
You were made in God's image. You have blood!
Life! Coursing through your veins.
Death spares you, so forgiveness will also.
Our time should be given to peace, and
If I refuse to war as an enemy,
Who should you in your resentment be,
Except for one's surrender I pray for.

The Love of Life

God loves you.
Sometimes
Experiencing
His love
Is birthed
By fight for
Survival.
Can happen near death,
Near quiet reflection,
To finally believe
God's word
Because you
Need too
Find yourself
Adored.
A babe in Him,
Understanding how sooner
His fathership,
Would have kept you
From
What questioned
Your worth
And caused
Your fight for Life.

Recurring Satisfaction

With a nature trail of beauties unknown, should we go back to yesterday? So much is left untold. It could be nice getting lost in the details—a thousand paths untaken, a thousand angles around the Lord, but He leads me in perfection, and of yesterday I know what I should. In every way, God gives recurring satisfaction.

Envisionings

1

Into the mystifying light!

Seek God's hand throughout your home—

Without sight, you'll feel His living presence,

As He stands in the place He's always promised.

A moment past humility, near the needy, by a prayer.

Though blind, you'll find everything—in knowing you are found.

2

Reach.
And please don't bother me.
God is more than faithful;
I have witnessed.
What you seek
Will be revealed.

3

Once,   by a dream,   I believe I witnessed
    A Spiritual portrait.
Only once,   and there was an eye   in the clouds.
And the sky   was painting colors   as it does at
              Sunset,
But the range of reds to purples   was in the vivid,
Pastel,   blooming   clouds themselves.

And wide,   center of the deep pigment   and
Brightly   hued   fluffing,
The eye pierces between rays of light   fluttering
Like lashes   and beaming waving luminance
Long over the soft   barrier line.

Caught in the wind and stare,   my sight,   too,
Strikes downward and lands,   hitting me in my bed
Where I am asleep,   dreaming these things.
Then I half wake,   attempting to assess:

    God's eye?   Was it supposed to be?   Is it?
                                   The living
    God.   God *is* real?
                Yes, of course.
I have a God!   We have a God.
All the world does!
All the world.   All people.

Do they know Him?
    Do they *KNOW* Him?
He *knows* us.
Our "unknown" God.
We have a great "unknown" God to be known.

Now I am up completely,   but still stammering
In switching thoughts.   I already knew I had a God.
He'd been leading me   (leads me)   and speaking
    To me often,
But seeing Him through a window,   a ceiling cage
Beneath His judgment,   an eye of justice...
    Frightening.
Except   He's told me not to fear   many times
    Before.   But I would;   I would reverence.
        The achievement?
A poetic explanation?
    A metaphor of how: my once clouded eyes
Never dreamed this way,   never envisioned God
Orchestrating   events day and night   for my faith.
Never had   a doorway   presenting the path
To walk   the narrow, straight;   for God to enter

    And introduce
Himself.   A King, on heights,   surreally rich.
A revelation;   teachings   under the "Great"
    Perspective.
I know not to fear anything in life   but Him.

    And His love is near,   is right beyond the veil.
Soon,
        And now,   betrothed,   I romanticize daily affairs.
      Eating   and drinking   are all accompanied,
                                      Glorious tasks,
    Are my grail of favor   brimming with
The sweetest wine.

A Simple Faith

God gives us sleep,
A simple faith.
Rest in all He's done.

Good News is true!
He can adopt you.
The Holy Spirit will take your hand.

And lead you to
Pasture and hill
Up to the *Heavenly home.*

Our, Father God,
Our Brother, Savior,
They who sent *Their* love,

Await to seal you in *Truine favor.*
Prepared for your arrival,
Your room is fresh and done.

Come and look
In *Their* presence
You will know.

You are family, His child!

Rooted in the heart!
You will not stray from truth.

Because He'll call to you
In kind rebuke;
This cry brings your return

To simple grace
Where the *inner lamp* sees
The Christ who's needed and does come.

Despite your doubtful
Tremoring soul
He'll take you up in arms

To restore belief, as
He does not condemn but love.
To His children, the kingdom belongs.

Embrace child-like,
Simple faith!
Our God grants us serenity.

Law of Liberty

My feet roam a land of liberty
Full of song and pride. Where
I honor the Lord who made me
And a love that never dies.
How granting love strips fear!
By Him my soul is endless.
My life is not my own but
Given to the hand of freedom.

Knight of Prayer

I found a knight who responds to His name
    uttered or thought.
Jesus came clothed in unbreakable armor
    I did not know to wear.
Prepared and unshakeable, above life's deception—
Knew nearing darkness, and did not hide,
But the Savior from serpents who prey on the blind
Who know only to lift a prayer in hope
    it reaches God at night.

Love Against Division

Don't be irrational
If someone hated you
Wouldn't they show it

Don't exclude yourself
Before rejection

Love is the way
Against divisions
Cut believing lies

Bond together
With what is true

Silence demons
Hope in Christ
No one else is perfect

Think the best
Grow fearless faith

Love is the way
Repentance
Graced

No Myths

Though flesh may boast my Spirit knows every good I know is grace.

Off haughty thoughts, no tempting plots, or sweet whisperings.

I will thank the Lord, who I love, and seek to know Him better.

What is the proper way? How can I logically feel towards Him?

If it sounds right, it must be? But what of wrong influence?

No friend or witch will control my hand. I won't be led astray,

But follow the Holy Spirit. To proudly go leads to a fall, if going is not grounded.

What can I trust? What is His voice? His word will be my only guidance.

If I have not seen God I cannot sense Him; correction has assured me.

Who can silence Satan except for the One who fulfilled God's prophesies?

Christ experienced resurrection! What He rejects and what He approves *that*

I will follow after! When He says God alone is good I will seek His goodness

Knowing apart from Him none maintains a seamless walk.

Faith's Flowers

1

Search for God's goodness in every aspect,
    and you'll find it.
Take the rain, find a seed, and watch it grow.
You'll miss the chance to trust and never blossom
While wandering the wilderness of doubt.

2

No enemy of God's children goes unashamed.
Do you covet human pride or pride in Him?
Pride in who truly loves, then you'll see humans lie
And the ground flowering forget-me-knots,
And a world of apology due before they're gone.
God will honor the sacrifice of the sower.
Amid the faith of His people, His splendor is born.

The Light in the Dark

I can ask why life leaves me in the dark
Or I can be lost in love.

God has taught me we don't need answers
For continuous questions—

Rather the retrieval of the all-around solution
In communion with Him.

THANK YOU

Dear reader,

Thank you so much for supporting this collection of prose and poetry. I pray that your faith has been edified, refreshed, and encouraged! The grace of God is a continuous blessing, an available mercy through Christ for anyone to receive at any moment of hearing and believing, and I desire your journey in Him to be one full of these great revelations!

Writing is an opportunity! I appreciate sharing my story and all that God has given me to know, do, and express. I thoroughly enjoy it and these thoughts of you.

All glory to God!, Janae Ballard

ABOUT THE AUTHOR

"Over The Rainbow" is a book of prose and poetry by Janae Ballard, a Christian young adult writing South in the United States. Owner of Heart of Glory Publishing, Janae is passionate to introduce various topics of growth, relationships, pain, and unique joy with a base of faith.

Find Janae's other resources, and published works at www.ballardjanae.com , also visit and discover details on future releases and more information about her artistry.

www.ingramcontent.com/pod-product-compliance
Lightning Source LLC
Chambersburg PA
CBHW071244070526
44583CB00017B/2321